À mon cher ami
Ch - Widor, ma...

affectueuse...

[signature]   22 - Nov. 1928

THE OLD HALL OF
LINCOLN'S INN

VIEW OF THE OLD HALL 1928

FROM A DRAWING BY F. W. KNIGHT

THE OLD HALL LINCOLN'S INN
F. W. KNIGHT

Frontispiece

SOME ACCOUNT OF THE OLD HALL OF LINCOLN'S INN

BY SIR JOHN W. SIMPSON, K.B.E.

ARCHITECT TO THE HONOURABLE
SOCIETY OF LINCOLN'S INN

'*Quis est enim, quem non moveat clarissimis monumentis testata consignataque antiquitas.*' Cic. Div. I

BRIGHTON: THE DOLPHIN PRESS
M. CM. XXVIII.

1928.

Made and printed in Great Britain by the
Dolphin Press, 10 Spring Gardens, Brighton

TO THE
TREASURER AND
MASTERS OF THE BENCH
OF THE
HONOURABLE SOCIETY OF
LINCOLN'S INN

PREFACE.

THE history of the building now known as the 'Old' Hall of Lincoln's Inn is, like that of many London buildings, very obscure. When Sir William Dugdale, Chester Herald and afterwards Garter King-of-Arms, wrote his 'Origines Juridiciales,' in 1666, he gave the substance of such information as he had found in the ancient Registers of the Inn, the 'LIBER HOSPICII DE LINCOLSIN' commonly known as the 'Black Books.' They contain, unfortunately, few references to the Hall and those but scanty. Although four quarto volumes of these and other records have now been published, they tell us little more of its early history than Dugdale knew. Much of their original text has, it is true, been condensed, but the earlier entries down to 1506 are set out 'substantially at length' and it is improbable that the careful labour of Mr. Paley Baildon left untranscribed any matter of importance anterior to that date. It is to be hoped that some competent palæographer may, before long, prepare a full transcript of these precious documents and make them available to students of London history. As regards the later history of the buildings of Lincoln's Inn, during the sixteenth, seventeenth, and eighteenth centuries, I cannot but think that rich treasure still awaits discovery.

Other documentary sources have proved as disappointing as the Black Books. Despite the help of so specially competent an antiquary as the late Mr. C. L. Kingsford, editor of Stow's 'Survey,' I have found no description of the Old Hall, nor any view of it earlier than the end of the eighteenth century, in the Library, the Print Room, or the Manuscript Department, of the British Museum. On early maps, such as those of Van den Wyngaerde (1550) and Ralph Agas (1560), or even Hollar's 'view' of 1648, the indications are too vague, or too obviously inaccurate, to be of much use. Neither the Record Office nor the Guildhall Library, nor the collections of Sir John Soane, the London Library, the London County Council and the London Society, nor the Libraries of Lincoln's Inn and of the Royal Institute of British Architects, appear to contain any records of this building.

The chronicle of its more recent history is almost as meagre as that of its early years. The wide field of contemporary notes and articles in the eighteenth and early nineteenth centuries—the 'European,' 'Gentleman's,' 'Town and Country,' and 'London,' Magazines—yields little or nothing from its hundreds of close-printed volumes. For time out of mind a fine piece of Tudor work has existed in the heart of London, unnoticed —forgotten.

In view, therefore, of the difficulties I have found in establishing the earlier history of the Hall, I have thought it well to place on record an account of this interesting building as I found it, and of the work which has been done by the Society's workmen in repairing it.

J.W.S.

CONTENTS

LIST OF ILLUSTRATIONS

I. ITS ANTIQUITY.

I.

ITS ANTIQUITY.

WHEN, in 1922, the Honourable Society of Lincoln's Inn held their Quingentenary celebration they commemorated, not their foundation but, merely the date on which their Records begin. In 1422 they were already paying annual rent to the Bishop of Chichester[1] and others for the property they now hold. Before that time, Mr. Williams[2] believes them to have been domiciled on the south side of Holborn, between Staple Inn and Barnard's Inn, where stood the 'Lyncolnesynne' of Thomas de Lincoln, King's Serjeant, whose occupation of it began in 1331. It was partly, if not wholly, inhabited by Clerks of Chancery and law-students. Thence, as it would appear, the Society removed in 1422, or a little earlier,

---

[1] At that time Thomas Polton, who had been Bishop of Hereford, and was translated in 1421 to the see of Chichester, which he held till his second translation to Worcester, in 1425-6.

[2] 'Early Holborn and the Legal Quarter of London,' by E. Williams, F.R.G.S., 2 vols. 4to. 1927.

19

to their present quarters on the west side of the 'Newe Street,' now Chancery Lane. For how long they had then been in existence is still uncertain.

Tradition, however, associates the name of the Society with that of Henry de Lacy, Earl of Lincoln and Lord of the Manor of the Holeburn who, having purchased in 1286 the buildings of the Dominicans on the shores of the Fleet, in what is now Shoe Lane, is said to have gathered round him a large number of law students. Though no documentary confirmation has been found of this traditionary connection it is, at least, supported by the fact that the Lacy 'Lyon rampant' was carved over the Gate of the Inn as early as 1518[1]. It is significant too, that the College of Heralds included the same charge in the Arms granted to the Society about sixty years later.

The interest of this matter justifies a short digression. When Richard Kingsmill purchased the Inn freehold from Edward Suliarde on behalf of the Bench in 1580, he applied to the Heralds College for a

---

[1] A fact which was advanced in proof of his title by Richard Montague, Bishop of Chichester, when claiming part of the Inn property in 1635.

Grant of Arms[1], and obtained the blazon '*Az.* semée of Mill-rinds *or* on a dexter canton of the second a Lyon rampant *purpure.*' This very beautiful coat incorporates the charges on Kingsmill's own shield (three sable mill-rinds on a silver field) and thereby dates itself. Yet, the Inn continued to use the Lacy coat until 1700[2], when the Bench being desirous of placing the arms of the Society on a piece of presentation plate, applied to the Heralds' Office for an 'authentick certificate' thereof. According to the Black Books[3] they then learned that 'by an ancient manuscript in the Library' (whether of the Inn or of the Heralds' College is not stated) their proper coat of arms was that above given. This 'ancient manuscript'— which cannot be found—is said to have traced the coat back to 1516, whereas Kingsmill was not admitted until 1543, and did not become a Bencher until 1558. The

---

[1]Williams (*op. cit.* §35).

[2]Dugdale, who was Norroy King of Arms in 1671, actually figures this coat as that of Lincolns Inn (Jurid. p.309) though Guillim, who was Rouge Croix Pursuivant in 1619, had given it correctly in his 'Display of Heraldry,'

[3]Vol. III. pp. 207, 208.

date 1516 appears to be a pen-slip for 1615 and to attach to a conversation (quoted by Howes in his 'Annales,'[1] printed in that year) between Sir George Buc and Chief Justice Sir George Lea, about the end of the XVI century. The latter then stated, quite correctly, that 'there was lately a coate deuised for this house' (*i.e.* some twenty years before), and recited the blazon obtained by Kingsmill.

As to the Lacy tradition, Mr. Williams' researches[2] lead him to the conclusion that a settlement of Chancery Clerks and Apprentices of the Courts existed, on the site of the present Inn, from the time of King Henry the Third's Lord Chancellor, Ralph de Neville, before Henry de Lacy was born. This Society and that of the Temple were originally one, and not until the latter was divided, in 1336, did the Bishop of Chichester's Inn, the Middle Temple, and the Inner Temple, becomes separate entities. The

---

[1] 'The Annales or Generall Chronicles of England begun first by Maister John Stow and after him continued and augmented with Matters forreyne and domestique unto the end of this present yeere 1614. By Edmond Howes, gentleman, Londini, impensis Thomae Adams, 1615.'

[2] op. cit. (§37. 38. 39).

Bishop's Inn was, it is said, absorbed into the Society of Lincoln's Inn, and took their name, at the time of the migration from Holborn in 1422.

It is impossible to speak with certainty of these early annals. While our gratitude is due to those who have devoted time and ability to the subject, we have to admit that nothing is known of the origin of the Society, or of the ancient topography of their buildings. Here, in the heart of London, lies an unworked mine for the skilled palæographer. The history of the great juridical foundation of Lincoln's Inn has yet to be written.

* * *

Forming part of the property acquired by the Society, when they established themselves in Chancery Lane, were the buildings which Chancellor Ralph de Neville, Bishop of Chichester, had erected to house the Clerks of his Chancery when he built his 'noble palace' early in the XIII century. They included a Hall and a Chapel, with Bakery, Brewery, and other appurtenances proper to the Clerks' lodgings. All these were probably timber structures, such as still survive at Staple Inn, except, perhaps, the Chapel to which portions of a stone doorway unearthed in 1877 are thought to have belonged. That neither the original Hall nor the Chapel stood upon the site of the present one is clear, though their actual position is uncertain. An entry in the Records for 1454, which speaks of glass windows having been placed at the 'east-end,' might justify the assumption that the first Hall stood east and west; but the phrase used is not conclusive, since there are also references to the 'east end' of the present hall, meaning it is clear, merely the eastern 'part,' or 'side.' The axis of the existing Hall lies nearly north and south, N.16°W. by S.16°E.

Heckethorn[1] asserts that until the erection of the Chancery Lane Gate-house the entrance to Lincoln's Inn was from Holborn. He gives no authority for this statement and its accuracy is improbable. The property to the north of the Inn fronting Holborn never belonged to the Bishops of Chichester or their successors. No road of access through it has been identified, nor would there seem to have been any need for one. The 'Newe Street,' now Chancery Lane, was formed by the Knights Templar as early as 1161, and

[1]'Lincolns Inn Fields and the Localities adjacent' London. 1896. 4to.

must always have been the natural frontage of the Inn property. But if such an entrance can be shown to have existed, it would conform the belief already referred to that the first Bishop's Hall stood east and west, since a 'screens' passage lay nearly always in the direction of the gateway. Great significance was attached to its being a traffic way, and Fulke Fitz-Warine, in the XIII century, is said to have caused the highway itself to pass through his hall so that nobody should escape his hospitality.

A side road—still indicated by Bishops Court, Portugal Street, and the now closed passage from Serle Street to New Square— ran from Chancery Lane to Drury Lane. To this road opened the postern gate of the Inn at the south-western corner of the ancient building, erected in 1535, now known as 13 New Square.

For some seventy years the Bishop's Hall served for the purposes of the Society. By 1489-90, however, it had fallen so far into decay that an order was made for it to be pulled down and a new Hall built. Sir Wm. Dugdale[1] says that the work was not begun until 1493 and thereafter proceeded,

[1]'Origines Juridiciales,' 1666. fol.

as it appears, so slowly that fourteen years
had passed before it was finished in 1507.
He has, however, confused the completion
of the Hall, which is known to have been
occupied in 1494, with that of the Council
room and Library building, which adjoined
it to the west and north and was erected in
1507. We find four students fined 10s. each
in the winter of 1492 for 'pulling down'
the derelict hall, doubtless—poor men—for
firing. No fire was provided in the Hall
before the Eve of All Saints (November 1st),
until 1684 when, 'the season being very
cold and fires needfull,' this Spartan regu-
lation was relaxed, and order made[1] that
'fires be made at Meales in the Hall and
that afterwards they be made and continued
in every succeeding Michaelmas Terme from
the beginning thereof.' Shocking to relate,
one of the Benchers also was guilty of pulling down part of the old building, and was
amerced in four marks for the offence. It
took him four terms to pay it, a mark (13s.
4d.) at a time, and we can but hope that
he got value for his money. The new Hall
of the Society was, as their Records show,
built in 1490-2.

---

1 'Black Books.' vol. III. p. 148.

We are writing, then, of a building erected in the very year when Columbus discovered America. Magellan had not then found the south-west passage to China and India, nor Vasco de Gama the shorter course around the Cape of Storms. Half a century was yet to pass before the coming of the Reformation. The Masters of the Bench of Lincoln's Inn had sate at the dais table in their Hall for forty years when Henry VIII began the Great Hall of Hampton Court; for a hundred years or ever Drake put out to smite the Spanish Armada.

It is older, by half a century, than any existing Hall of the other Inns of Court and Chancery. That of Gray's Inn 'as it now standeth' was begun, according to Dugdale, in 1557 and finished in 1560; while the Hall of the Middle Temple was not built until 1572. The date of Staple Inn Hall is 1581, and that of Clifford's Inn very much later.

II. ITS EARLY HISTORY.

II.

ITS EARLY HISTORY

OUR forefathers were not troubled with
the fretful eagerness to depart from
tradition that troubles the designers of our
day. Having discovered by experiment a
form of dwelling that satisfied their needs,
they were content to reproduce it, with such
decorative variations only as expressed the
taste of the period in which they lived.
Hence, the arrangement of the Hall and its
accessory Offices, which were the centre of
English domestic life, persisted without
material change for more than three hundred years. Almost invariably they were so
placed as to divide the Outer Court with its
Gate-House, from the Inner Court; com-
munication between the two Courts being
provided by the passage-way known as 'the
Screens.' Their disposition may be stated

diagrammatically thus:—

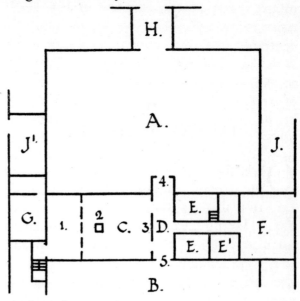

A. *Outer Court.*
B. *Inner Court.*
C. *Hall.* 1. *Dais.* 2. *Fireplace.* 3. *Screen.*
D. *'The Screens' (with gallery over).* 4. *Porch.* 5. *Door to B.*
E.E. *Panetry and Buttery.*
E¹. *Surveying Place (Servery).*
F. *Kitchen.*
G. *Withdrawing Room (with 'Solar' over).*
H. *Gate-House.*
J. *Lodgings.*
J¹. *Chapel (position variable but generally near dais).*

32

A projecting bay window was very commonly built at the dais end of the Hall; more rarely two such bays are found. The central hearth, over which was a roof turret with slatted openings (louvres) to allow the smoke to escape, was replaced, in course of time, by a fireplace and chimney in one of the side walls. An undercroft, or cellar, under the Kitchen and Offices, and sometimes under the Hall itself, was often provided for storage of food, wine and fuel. It is not unusual to find the Hall floor raised several feet above the level of the courtyards, in order to give light and ventilation to this undercroft.

Even in the seventeenth century the national screen and passage-way plan still survived, until our own traditions yielded to the continental influence of a classic renaissance.

It was precisely in this typical form that the Hall of Lincoln's Inn was built, with a length of 60ft. and a width of 32ft.; its proportions being similar to that of the Hall of the Bishop's Palace at Hatfield, of which further mention will be made. Two Bay windows opened, from the east and west ends of the raised dais[1] at the upper end, under deli-

---

[1] 'att the hyghe dease' ('Black Books' Nov. 19th, 1546).

cately moulded stone arches. These arches, of very gracious curve, were carried on corbels in the likeness of winged angels displaying shields. Each Bay had two storeys of mullioned lights, their cills being carried down nearly to the floor, and the heads enriched with flat pointed arches at both the transom and upper levels. South of the bays were three windows on either side of the Hall, each of three lights, the cills of which were about ten feet from the floor. Below them ran magnificent 'linen-fold' oak panelling of the same design—very possibly by the same hand—as that of Cardinal Wolsey's Ante-Chamber at Hampton Court Palace which was being built about the same time. The floor was paved either with stone or, like that of the Hall of Hampton Court[1], with tiles, and was strewn thickly every day with fresh rushes, or straw. In view of the rough manners of mediæval times, it was desirable to have a surface which could be frequently and quickly washed down. Clean loose straw, how-ever has always temptation for lively Youth, and fines are recorded for throwing it about during meal-times. 'Quia jactavit wippiss' cost

---

[1] This famous Hall having like its earlier fellow of Lincoln's Inn, fallen into decay, has also by a coincidence undergone thorough structural repair at the same time.

INTERIOR OF THE OLD HALL 1928

BY THE COURTESY OF "THE TIMES"

masters Parker, Norwich, Mynors, Froxmer, Carewe, Batemanson, Forcette, and Metford 12d. a piece[1] and, incidentally, preserved their names for all time. Norwich, to be sure, rose to the dignity of 'Serjeant' and Mynors became a Bencher; irrepressible Metford has many other fines to his name, while Froxmer's thin-spun life was slit two years later by the plague. But none of those 'yong Gentilmen' dreamed, when they 'ragged' among the oaken tables and the straw, that they were achieving an in-expensive (if worthless) immortality. This was in 1506, when the lads carried daggers. Their brawls were not always so harmless, and blood has been spilled often enough in the Hall of Lincoln's Inn.

In the early part of the seventeeth century (1624), the Hall was lengthened twelve feet by the addition of two southern Bays; copies, though somewhat inferior in detail, of those on the dais which formed part of the original struc-ture. At the northern angle of the eastern of these later Bays, parts of the stone jamb of the first entrance doorway from the Gate-House court[2]

---

[1]'Black Books,' vol, 1, pp. 141, 143.

[2]The quadrangle next Chancery Lane, now known as 'Old Buildings,' was still in the XVIII. century called 'Gate-house Court.'

to the Screens has been uncovered, and is now exposed to view. Opposite to it, on the west side, the doorway to the Inner court has been found almost intact, with the old hooks for the hinge-straps still in position and now again in use. One of its arch-stones was unfortunately damaged in 1911, when cutting an opening through the modern brickwork in which it was concealed[1], but this has been successfully repaired and replaced. Of the ancient Screen no traces remain, but it is known that a gallery, 'for the surplusage of the company of this Howse,' and for 'musick,' was built over it in 1565. That now in position at the lower end dates from 1624, when £40 was paid 'to Robert Lynton joiner for the new skreen in the Hall.'[2] It is not a true Screen, but a frontispiece to the south wall, and is wrought only on one side. The happy proportions and grouping of the features of this fine specimen of Renaissance

---

[1] Mr. Paley Baildon states ('Country Life,' Dec. 16th, 1922) quite erroneously, that half the doorway was broken to fragments. Bellot repeats and embroiders this error by asserting that 'it was broken up by the workmen owing to the negligence of the person in charge of the works.' The stones were on the contrary, preserved 'in situ' and a glass panel was formed in the wall by which they could be inspected.

[2] 'Black Books,' vol. II. p. 253.

woodwork reveal the hand of a master. Its Jacobean detail may be, most likely is, that of Lynton the joiner. But, the general design from which he worked was probably that of Inigo Jones, who was engaged on the adjoining Chapel at the time it was made. Though no drawing of it can be found in the Burlington and Devonshire collections, the view here expressed is also that of Mr. Gotch, F.S.A., an undoubted authority on the great architect and his work.

On stripping from this screen the countless coats of paint and imitation oak 'graining' which covered it, it was found that parts of the original oak of the lower portion had been patched with deal, and some of the carved work replaced by composition. This iniquity may safely be laid to the account of those who mutilated the building at the end of the eighteenth century, of whom more will be presently told.

At the time the Hall was thus extended the original south wall was taken down and rebuilt in line with the new south Bays, the new Jacobean screen being fixed against it, and a 'screens' passage with new doorways formed in the position to which it has now been restored. The old east and west doors were bricked up, their very existence being forgotten and unsuspected until the discovery, already mentioned, of the latter in 1911. The cellar under this extension was made later and does not coincide with the earlier portions. Its vaulting, of which the axis is east and west instead of north and south like the rest, was only erected about 1888 to replace decayed joisting.

* * *

At the south end of the buildings were the Buttery and Panetry, the latter probably on the west side, with a passage-way between them leading to the Kitchen, which faced south towards the Kitchen Garden. These Offices were converted into chambers about 1845, but sufficient indications remain to make it probable that their original plan could be reconstituted by a careful survey. The 'gathering' of the Kitchen chimney from its hood is still visible, also the stair, now boarded over, connecting the Buttery to the cellar. The cellars, which extend under both the Hall and its Offices, are beautifully vaulted in brick on a three-centred arch section, and have semi-circular intersecting vaults to the window openings. Those under the Hall itself were formed when the extension was made in 1624, and follow in design those under the Offices which are about a century earlier in date.

Externally the walls were faced with red bricks, rather thinner and longer than those now made, four courses measuring eleven inches in height. Diapers of interlacing diamonds were formed of darker bricks which had caught the fire when being burned. Unlike modern imitations of Tudor work, where specially black and staring 'headers' have been used, these old patterns are but softly outlined, and enriched, without disturbing, the quiet wall surfaces. The bricks themselves closely resemble those used for both Hampton Court Palace and the Henry VIII Gate-House of the Inn, in Chancery Lane. On the eastern front the brick pattern is rather smaller than on the west, the diamond intersections of the latter occurring only every twelve courses in height, whereas on the former they occur at every eighth course with benefit to the scale of the building.

Without doubt the most interesting feature of the Hall is its fine open timber roof. As first built it comprised three massive arched cross frames (principals) of enormous timbers, with two half-frames at the north and south ends respectively. All these frames are still in position, but when the Hall was lengthened, c. 1624, the southern half-frame was doubled in thickness by the addition of a second half, whose mouldings differ from those of the original half, and clearly indicate its date. Another half-frame was then placed against the newly added south wall; but the old one at the north end still remains in its first state and position.

The three great cross-frames and their intermediate rafters appear to be even older than the horizontal purlins (longitudinal bearers) and the ogee-curved cusped wind-braces which connect them. They are technically 'scissor-framed braces,' whose upper lengths pass through the collar ties and are tenoned to the opposite principal rafter. At their crossings they are halved and secured, as are all the tenons, with stout oak trenails. No iron was used in constructing them. Part of a heavy wall-post was found attached to the back of one of the ancient braces and built, without use or apparent purpose, deep into the brickwork. This suggests that the couples (copulae) may be parts of an earlier timber structure, probably the first Hall of the Bishops of Chichester, which were re-used in the new buildings of 1492. The density of the oak of which they are made indicates its great antiquity. The curious wind-braces and purlins already mentioned are clearly of the same date as the walls.

In the roof of the fourteenth century church at Adderbury we find curved and cusped braces from the king-posts to the ridge-pieces. At Eltham palace the well known fifteenth century roof has ogee-curved wind-braces (sometimes called purlin-braces) but without cuspings. At Malvern Abbey, in the lower tier only, these braces are cusped, but are not ogee-curved. Moreover, the constructional design of these roofs differs altogether from that of the Hall of Lincoln's Inn. But there are remarkable resemblances between the last named building and the Hall of the Old Palace at Hatfield. Their open timber roofs are almost alike, both having scissor-brace couples without wall-posts and double tiers of ogee-curved wind-braces, which differ only by the absence at Hatfield of the cuspings which distinguish those of Lincoln's Inn. The span of the Hatfield roof is four feet less than that of the Inn, the length of both Halls being the same. Both buildings are of brick, with four-centred arched window lights, and buttresses with double weathered set-offs of similar outline. But whereas the Lincoln's Inn Hall has windows and weatherings of stone, those of the Hatfield Hall are of brick.

The erection of two sister roofs, which appear to have no like in England, at about the same time[1] and within twenty miles one of the other, cannot be accounted a mere coincidence. Hatfield Palace was built for John Morton, afterwards Cardinal archbishop of Canterbury who, after practising as a lawyer in the Court of Arches, became Master of the Rolls in 1473, and Lord Chancellor in 1487. In 1479 he had been elected Bishop of Ely, and dwelt—a stone's throw from Lincoln's Inn—at the episcopal palace in Ely Place, to whose famous fruit gardens Shakespeare refers in 'The Tragedy of King Richard the Third[2].' Morton was a notable builder. He had taken up archbishop's Bourchier's famous work at Knole, on that primate's death in 1486, and was busy with the gate-house and tower of Lambeth Palace when the Society were about to build their Hall. With his early training, and with such a bent, he would be much interested in the building scheme of his old neighbours at Lincoln's Inn, with whom

---

[1] Hatfield is some ten years the earlier of the two.
[2] *Gloucester*—When I was last in Holborn,
    I saw good strawberries in your garden
                                        there:
    I do beseech you send for some of them.
Ely—'Marry, and will, my Lord, with all my heart.'
                                (Act III. Scene 4).

42

HATFIELD OLD PALACE. ROOF OF THE HALL
BY THE COURTESY OF "COUNTRY LIFE"

he must pretty certainly have been acquainted, and in whose Chapel, he may have preached. Where a page of history is missing it is not unlawful to hazard a conjecture at its contents, provided it be in accord with contextual facts. It seems then—to complete the little fabric of assumption—more than likely that Chancellor Morton was consulted about the new Hall and that, highly pleased with the charming work of that kind he had done at Hatfield, he commended its designer to the Bench of Lincoln's Inn.

* * *

On Thursday, being the 'Nyne and Twentieth Day of February One Thousand Six Hundred Seaventy one'—as appears by the Admission Book of the Honourable Society—it pleased King Charles the Second, with Prince James, Prince Rupert, and 'diverse of the Nobilitie' to dine in the Hall. The King sitting at his table 'upon the assent att the upper end of the Hall and railed in,' was served by the Reader[1] as Server upon his Knee with the Towell before he did eate. The Dukes and Lords and other his Maties Attendants of Qualitie after some short time of waiting had leave from his Matie to sitt downe to Dinnar att Tables pre-

---

[1] Sir Francis Goodericke, the Solicitor-General.

pared for them. The Reader and some of the Benchers all the tyme of his Maties Dining waiteing neere his Maties Chaire and foure other of the Benchers with White Staffes waited as Controlers of the Hall to keepe good order and above fifty of the Barristers and Students the most parte of them attending as Waiters and carrieing up his Maties Meate.' The rest of the barristers and students waited upon the Lords, 'att theire Table.'

It would seem that neither benchers, barristers, nor students, had any part in the 'three courses wherein were exceeding great Plenty and variety of Dishes and after them a most liberall Banquett,' served up and delivered by them upon their knees. Since that February day, more democratic customs have crept into even the nicely regulated relations of the Crown and the Bar.

From the narrative which Lane has piously transcribed[1] emerges a point in the history of the Hall; for we learn that 'the Musick consisting of his Maties Violins was playing all the tyme of Dinnar in the Gallery att the lower end of the Hall.' There was, then, as might be expected, a gallery over the present passage-way

[1] 'The Student's Guide through Lincoln's Inn' (4th dition), London, 1823.

44

(the Screens) at the south end; this has now disappeared and its place become part of the chambers numbered 17 Old Buildings. About 1820 (according to Lane) the old openings from this Gallery to the Hall were filled with painted achievements of the Arms of King Charles II, H.R.H. James duke of York, H.S.H. Prince Rupert, the earls of Manchester and Bath, Lord Henry Howard, and Lord Newport, in commemoration of the Royal visit. These paintings, excellent specimens of the heraldic work of their time, have now been replaced in the position for which they were designed.

III. ITS LATER HISTORY.

III.
ITS LATER HISTORY.

DRASTIC changes were made in the latter years of the eighteenth century, when the Hall was ceiled with plaster vaulting suspended from the roof beams. Ireland[1], who died in 1800, says that 'the roof as it now appears, being plastered, is certainly of more modern date than the other parts of the building; and we have no doubt but that it was originally constructed of oak.' It is clear that this deplorable alteration had been made some years before his time. We find it shown in Rowlandson's view which Ackerman[2] published in 1808. Yet so quickly are matters of this kind forgotten, that Spilsbury[3], who was Librarian to the Inn and had access to the Records, could believe in 1850 that the ceiling had been erected only thirty years before he wrote.

---

[1] 'Picturesque views of the Inns of Court,' London, 1800.

[2] 'The Microcosm of London,' 3 vols., 4to, London, 1808-11.

[3] 'Lincoln's Inn, its ancient and modern buildings,' London, 1850.

At the time when Sir James Thornhill was painting the dome of Saint Paul's Cathedral with scenes from the life of the Patron saint, his son-in-law, Hogarth, was tempted to try his hand at the same subject. By a curious chance, his adventure in religious art was associated with the Hall of Lincoln's Inn.

According to Lane[1], 'Lord Wyndham, baron Finglass and Chancellor of Ireland, left by his will two hundred pounds to be expended in ornamenting the hall by any means the treasurer and benchers should approve. Lord Mansfield, who had an intimate acquaintance with, and personal esteem for, Hogarth, proposed that the two hundred pounds should be applied in the purchase of a painting by this celebrated artist, that they might at once perform the intention of the testator and encourage the fine arts. Hogarth painted the picture; and solicitous to learn if it met the approbation of the benchers waited upon them for that purpose, when he was invited to dine with them,—a favour seldom conferred but on legal or ecclesiastical characters, and generally members of the society.'

Mr. Paley Baildon[2] says that it was intended

---

[1] Op. cit.

[2] v. 'Country Life' supra.

for the Chapel; but the size of the picture, fourteen feet by ten feet six inches, indicates that it was painted for the Hall, where it was duly placed in 1750. Though the subject, 'Paul before Felix,' ingeniously combines forensic with religious interest, and the composition is admittedly fine, the work has been stigmatised as 'Hogarth's great failure.' It has been suggested by a cynical litigant that he attempted the impossible, the constituent ideas being incompatible.

From 1737 onwards the Hall was used, more or less continuously, for sittings of the Court of Chancery. In 1819 a Court for the Vice-Chancellor (a title now abolished) was built at the north-west angle of the Hall, extending to where the War Memorial now stands, with an arcade connecting it to the Hall. In 1841 a detached Court with a wooden loggia was erected to the East of the Hall, nearly filling the Gate-house quadrangle; this block is shown on the contemporary Ordnance maps. Both Courts were demolished in 1883.

As dinner in the XVIII century was at 4.30, the time being altered to 5 o'clock only in 1829, and it is known that the whole Hall but barely held the numbers dining, it would be interesting to know how it contrived to pay this double debt. Contemporary writers mention the fact of its being used as a Court, but give no hint of any inconvenience to the Inn being caused thereby. Ackerman's view shows fixed desks and tables for Counsel in the upper half of the Hall. Were the diners all crowded into the lower part, or was provision made for them elsewhere? The Court fittings could hardly have been cleared away and refixed daily.

It is asserted by several writers that the building was lengthened by ten feet in 1818, but this is certainly not true as regards the structure of the Hall. What then happened was that, being greatly in want of additional dining space, the Society formed a new passage-way at the south end, and incorporated the space occupied by 'the screens' of 1624 with the Hall. No alteration was made to the screen itself, but some extra mess tables were set, between the openings to the Hall and to the Offices, among which the servitors had to thread their way as best they might. It must have been an inconvenient arrangement, and the new and larger Hall built in 1843 was clearly needed. When the latter was completed the old Kitchen and Offices were converted into chambers, as No. 20 Old Buildings[1]; the first floor becoming No. 17, a number which had been missing since the alteration to Nos. 12 and 13 New Square in 1738.

To provide an entrance and staircase to the first floor of these chambers, the 'screens' passage of 1624 was again severed from the Hall, the openings in the Screen itself being filled in with sham 'four panel' deal doors, duly painted and grained. The Gallery over seems to have disappeared in 1818, being annexed to the chambers adjoining. Its quasi-arcade which looked upon the Hall was blocked up, and the openings filled (in 1820) with the painted achievements already described, which commemorate the Royal visit of 1671.

Though the work of the fifteenth century had been sound and good, that at the end of the eighteenth century was disastrous for the historic Hall as regards both design and execution. It would seem that the insertion of the plaster ceiling and the reckless mutilations of the roof-timber frames which accompanied it, without regard to the additional load inflicted on them, had caused them to push the

---

[1] Afterwards No. 21 and now 17: the numbering varies according to the sets of chambers with which the old rooms are let from time to time.

ancient walls outwards. In order to counter-
act that movement the old buttresses were
pulled down, being cut away to the wall line
(where the original bonding has been found)
and new and wider ones built. This work was
done as unskilfully as the rest, the new buttresses not being 'toothed' or tied in any way
to the walls, but merely placed against them
with a 'straight joint.' Built of thick stock-
bricks of poor quality, they were mingled
with lumps of chalk, and fragments of stone
from the Tudor parapet, which was likewise
demolished and rebuilt with a clumsy battlemented coping of 'Parker's' cement. The
stonework of the windows was dreadfully
maltreated. Iron nails about six inches long
were hammered into the mortar joints, and
even into the stone itself which was ruthlessly
split and mutilated. Prodigious quantities of
string having been twined about and between
the nails, the whole surface of the stone and
brickwork (except the face of the eastern wall)
was covered thickly with Parker's cement.
The window mullions were coarsely remould-
ed in this material (then newly invented),
and trefoil cuspings added to their arched
heads; the openings were adorned with heavy
hood-moulds, the old leaded-lights with their

VIEW OF THE OLD HALL IN 1805

FROM A DRAWING BY S. RAWLE

wrought ironwork cleared away, and the windows all glazed with large sheets of glass.

Inside, the fair oak panelling was replaced by painted deal framing, probably considered more in accord with the ceiling. The Jacobean screen of oak was allowed to remain, but was duly 'painted and grained' to correspond with the new woodwork.

According to Heckethorn[1] these drastic alterations excited the indignation of experts; 'the compo was much objected to at the time, especially as it speedily peeled off.' It must certainly have been many times renewed, for when the walls were stripped for examination, they were found to be coated with layers of cement to the thickness of four to six inches.

But however forcibly the 'indignation of experts' may have been expressed, it left the Benchers of the time unmoved. In June 1818, as the Black Books record, 'the following repairs etc. were ordered:—The roof of the Hall to be repaired, and a new cupola erected over it . . . . the east side of the Hall to be stuccoed to correspond with the west side.' A huge new 'cupola' ornate with

---

[1] *See also* 'The Gentleman's Magazine,' 1807, No. LXXVII. 1812, No. LXXXII.

pinnacles, crockets, and tracery, was accordingly concocted of deal and plaster, and the oaken 'loover,' which had stood since the time of Edward VI, disappeared. The tiling was removed from the roof, and slating substituted. These final degradations having been inflicted on the unfortunate building, it was painted all over—walls, parapets, windows and turret—a monotonous and funereal drab.

Work of this sort is not kindly treated by Time, especially in London town. Under clearer skies decay may be turned to beauty, or hidden, by Nature's pleasant growths. But the condition of the venerable Hall of Lincoln's Inn had, by the early years of the present century, become most lamentable. Sooty deposits defined every blemish, and a network of blackened fissures spread upon its surface like a grimy blight. Thick with paint, disfigured, and decrepit, it was wholly unlovely of aspect both without and within.

Who was responsible for those criminal doings of the XVIII century? Official records are discreetly silent as to his name; but we may guess it to have been James Wyatt who, 'restoring' *more suo* in 1790-6, removed the timber roof from the Chapel and, there too, substituted a plaster ceiling. On this work he is known to have employed one Bernasconi, doubtless an expert at the dreadful business of string and stucco. Spilsbury openly charges him with the work at the Hall, and there can be little doubt of his guilt, for the stonework of the Chapel windows has been dealt with in like manner to that of the Hall, where would seem to have been committed the earlier, and probably experimental, offence. He, was, at any rate, but an accessary of Wyatt, whose handiwork at certain cathedrals has left such a reputation as even his misdeeds at Lincoln's Inn cannot smirch. Wyatt, moreover, was co-inventor with Parker of the cement he used so lavishly!

IV. ITS REPAIR.

IV.
ITS REPAIR.

IN 1924—four hundred and thirty years after its erection—the architect to the Bench reported that the Hall, whose condition had caused him anxiety for several years, was showing signs of imminent collapse. The glass, tightly cemented in the window openings, was constantly cracking and there were many other indications of a movement being in progress. The roof slating had so completely perished that rain penetrated it freely, and it was necessary to add a temporary covering of felt. It was, in fact, clear that the life of the building, greatly shortened by the mutilations of the eighteenth and nineteenth centuries, was nearly at an end.

It was felt by the Benchers that to pull down a building so closely connected with the history of their Inn or, alternatively, to invest it with a system of shores and struts in order to preserve it as an interesting, but useless, archæological relic, were both inadmissible propositions. On the other hand, to attempt to 'restore' the Hall to its original state was impracticable, because of the structural changes which have been described, and purposeless, in view of the fact that Hardwick's new Hall of 1843 now provides for the domestic life of the Inn. At best, too, such a procedure could result only in a more or less successful copy of the original building. Order was therefore made for the execution, step by step, of a thorough structural repair, in order to render it once more fit for occupation, while preserving all that was possible of the old work. It is in accordance with this principle of repair—as opposed to 'restoration'—that the works now completed have been carried out.

*   *   *

Some exploratory opening-up of the structure was first undertaken, with gratifying results. It was found that the cement, with which the walls had been so plentifully coated, could be stripped from the walls without injuring their faces. The first layer had been applied, as it would seem, without soaking the ancient bricks sufficiently to ensure its adhesion, and there was but little difficulty in cleaning them. As a beginning, a portion of the eastern wall about ten feet square was exposed, and its diaper-patterning brought

PLAN OF THE OLD HALL AS EXISTING (1928).

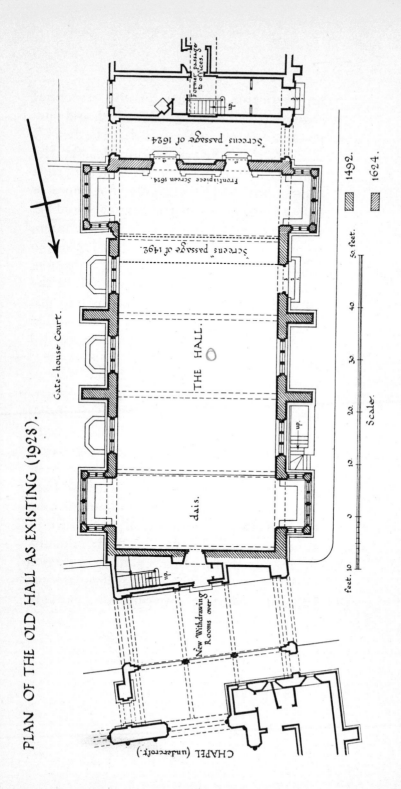

V

Gate-house Court.

"Screens" passage of 1492.

"Screens" passage of 1624.

Frontispiece Screen 1624.

Former passage to offices.

up.

THE HALL.

dais.

up.

up.

New Withdrawing Rooms over.

CHAPEL (undercroft.)

1492.

1624.

feet. 10   0   10   20   30   40   50. feet.

Scale.

once more to light after being hidden for a century and a half. Few things happen in London which escape the observant activity of the Press. Within an hour of its disclosure the reporter of an evening paper was seeking information from the architect about this unknown piece of Tudor brickwork, which had caught his eye as he passed along Chancery Lane.

Examination of the stonework proved less satisfactory, for removal of the stucco casing disclosed grievous damage. Not only had it suffered the horrible mutilations already described, but decay—evidently in progress before the cement was applied—had continued beneath its surface. In some parts no more than an inch square of stone remained of what had once been solid mullions; and the utmost care was needed, when taking apart the windows for repair, to prevent them from collapsing in ruin. The internal faces and their mouldings were, however, on the whole in fairly good condition.

The stone which the fifteenth century masons had used, was identified by the Geological Survey Board as of the upper Greensand formation, known as Gatton, Reigate, or Merstham, stone. Not very durable even in favourable conditions, the foolish destruction of its outer protecting, or 'weathered' face, when preparing it for stucco, had accelerated the kind of bacterial decay to which, in common with many other soft stones, it is liable. It was a favourite material with mediæval masons[1]. Sir Christopher Wren in his 'Memorial' of 1713[2] on the condition of Westminster Abbey, says of this stone—*I find, after the Conquest, all our artists were fetched from Normandy; they loved to work in their own Caen-stone, which is more beautiful than durable. This was found expensive to bring hither, so they thought Rygate-stone in Surrey, the nearest like their own, being a stone that would saw and work like Wood, but not durable.* He adds that, *good Stone gathers a Crust, and defends itself, as many of our English Free-stones do.*

It was clear to the Architect that the roof, which had spread considerably, was still pushing the walls out of perpendicular, and that the ill-built buttresses offered but inadequate resistance to its thrust. Stress diagrams, which were set up by calculation, showed the utmost limit

---

[1] The Liberate Roll of 35, Henry III. contains an order to the Sheriff of Surrey and Sussex to 'repair the pillars of our hall at Guildford with good Reigate stone'

[2] 'Parentalia,' part II. sec. VII.

of stability to have been reached, insomuch that the structure might fall without further warning than the signs of distress already observed had given. The plaster vault was found to be quite rotten, and heavily coated with mildew fungus due to dampness and lack of ventilation and light.

Although it had been ascertained—by hazardous crawling with candles beneath the slating —that this vaulting was suspended from the oak frames of an old roof, it was not until its many tons of plaster, laths, bearers, and clumsy joisting, had been cleared away that the actual form and condition of the carpentry they concealed could be seen and examined. Few, even of those whose lives are concerned with building, have been privileged to bring to light an unrecorded open-timber roof of the fifteenth century. None of those who saw the curves and mouldings of its mighty members come forth, as the clotted stucco in which they had so long been buried fell away in clouds of dust and filth, will forget that dramatic resurrection.

Except for a few missing, or broken, windbraces and the greater part of a trefoiled cornice-board, the roof was found to be complete. Most of its injuries had been caused by the insertion of the misconceived ceiling, when the great timbers had been ruthlessly cut and hacked to receive deal bearers and joisting. Its dislocation was, however, appalling. With few exceptions all the oaken trenails were shorn through and, the members having consequently parted company, the couples had lost all cohesive formation. In 1889, the principal rafters—solid timbers about a foot and a half square weighing several tons—had been bored to receive heavy iron tie-bars, evidently in the hope of arresting the spreading movement. Exposure showed these bars to have been quite useless, for they had been bolted, not to the timbers they were intended to secure but to the parapets, the thinnest and weakest parts of the wall. Perhaps the most abominable mutilation of all was inflicted in 1818, at the time when slating was substituted for the old tiling. A distortion of the ridge level, the sign by which the unfortunate roof proclaimed its distress under the extra load imposed upon it by the groined ceiling, seems to have offended the eyes of those in charge. The means which they adopted to restore it to a straight line are almost incredible. A length of about three feet was sawn off the upper ends of all the rafters, as well as of the principals themselves, and the ridge-piece removed, thus destroying the important apical connections of the framework. The addition of a flat upper roof effectually hid the mischief which had been done. That the roof still continued to exist, instead of falling in pieces on the heads of the Lord Chancellor and his court, is an astounding tribute to the work of its Tudor builders.

* * *

Having, as has been told, relieved the roof of its load of sham vaulting, the next step was to remove the weight of the roof itself from the walls, and to repair it. Before doing so a temporary roof was erected over the whole building to protect it from further damage by the weather; a precaution which should always be taken when an ancient structure is being opened up for repair.

The roof was then taken apart, after careful drawings had been made showing each constituent piece of timber, and a number painted on each piece corresponding with its reference on the index drawings. There was thus no risk of the parts being confused or wrongly placed during re-erection. Some damage to the timbers had been done by wood-beetles, especially in the dark and unventilated spaces at their feet where they had been covered by plaster-work; the wall-plate was, indeed, completely destroyed. The late Professor Lefroy was consulted about this trouble and, by his advice, all the wood-work was well sprayed, before it was disturbed, with a preparation of which he supplied the formula. As such beetles take their flight in Spring, a second spraying was given to the separated parts at the begining of the year (1926), after they had been taken down, in order to prevent infection being carried to the woodwork of other buildings in the neighbourhood. The Professor's treatment was effective; no living grubs or beetles have ever been discovered since the spraying was done. It must have been almost the last work he did, outside the laboratory, before his lamented death.

Preparations to lower the southernmost roof-couple revealed that at some time (with or without the knowledge of the Bench!) the brickwork of the head wall above the false ceiling had been removed by an ingenious tenant of the adjoining chambers, who added useful space to his kitchen by building out a lath and plaster partition upon the principal itself. Here was a quite unsuspected risk of fire, which the old roof had escaped with the many other hazards of its neglected age.

More interesting was the discovery that beneath the dilapidated 'cupola' of painted deal and plaster erected in 1818 existed the original eight-sided oak 'loover' or 'lanthorn' which was renewed[1] after the 'great wind' of January in the fifth year of Edward VI (1551). Its framework, which seems to be coeval with the earlier roof timbers, and the shaped rafters of its dome proved to be still perfectly sound, and all the parts were duly indexed and set aside for re-erection.

No 'rubbish' should ever be removed from an ancient building until it has first been carefully examined. Owing to this precaution some of the ancient roof-tiles were found; rather thinner and narrower than those now currently made and of an excellent quality. Portions of the original iron window-stan-cheons with their forged cross-bars were also rescued, together with some of the old lead cames and lead-ribbon ties of the ancient glazing. Most interesting of all, the boarded crawling-way above the ceiling was found to consist of very beautiful linen-fold panelling. Put together, it formed a wainscot about nine feet high, which had been evidently the

---

[1]'Black Books,' vol. 1. p. 302.

early lining of the Hall; unfortunately, enough only remained to furnish one severy width, and that much injured by misuse. It is difficult to understand why such valuable work should have been pulled down, unless on the theory already suggested, that it was thought by Wyatt to conflict in character with his plastered vault. Horace Walpole may have carried it off in triumph to Strawberry Hill, where its beauty would at least have been appreciated. A like story is told about the lovely work of Grinling Gibbons at Winchester, during the aesthetic fury of the gothic revival.

An offer of oak several centuries old having been made to the Council of the Inn, it was decided to accept it, and to re-construct with this material the missing portions of the panelling.

The immense strain to which the disparted roof timbers had been improperly subjected, was shown by their having taken a permanent 'set.' Not only the stout oak rafters but, incredible to relate, the huge principal beams had *bent* from four to six inches in their length. A common device of carpenters for restoring warped timber to its true plane is the saturation of the inner curve with moisture while heat is applied to dry the outer.

70

To this end, experimental grooves were cut in some of the roof members and filled with water, in the hope that it would penetrate and soak the exposed fibres. So close, however, had their texture become by age that no absorption whatever could be observed; the wood held water like a metal pot. Nor could any deflection be obtained, even under great pressure. It was, obviously, not possible to push this test too far, lest the timber should split along its grain and so be ruined.

It was therefore decided to resort to surgery. Two long and deep mortices were cut, thus:— midway in the length of a beam. Pressure by screw-  jacks from a steel girder was then applied, very slowly, until the wood fibres cracked across their grain, at the points on the weakened line a—a, and so allowed the beam to straighten. The mortice cuts (shown by the darker portions of the section) were then filled with accurately worked splices of oak, about three hundred years old, and these were secured by trenails driven through the whole thickness of the beam. The operation proved entirely successful, the old timbers being left as strong as they had ever been, or stronger.

A very slight adzing of the backs brought them to a line sufficiently true to receive oak feather-edged fillets, of which the upper side took the tiling-pegs, while the underside ceiled the rafters. To make all doubly safe a wrought iron heel-strap was passed round the back of each principal, where it was out of sight, and bolted to the cross-ties. There is little fear of their moving again for many centuries to come.

The posts, rafters, and framework, of the ancient 'lanthorn' being sound and perfect were refixed, its roof boarding replaced and covered with copper, and sufficient louvre boards inserted for ventilation.

* * *

As regards the stonework, its deplorable condition has already been described. But though the external faces were hopelessly decayed, where they had not been destroyed, the internal portions were fairly sound. All these were scrupulously preserved, each stone being numbered before it was taken down and its position accurately recorded on large-scale drawings. After removing the decayed portions, the old stones were reinforced by dowelling on to them a new external face of Portland stone, specially selected from the famous Saint Paul's quarry. The stones of the ancient western doorway, discovered in 1911, were but slightly affected by decay, and two coats of hot limewash proved an effective remedy. Some hesitation was felt about applying it lest it should obliterate some traces of incised lettering on the jamb-stones, probably the work of idle apprentices long since dead. Careful rubbings were first taken of these 'sgraffiti' which the officials of the Record Office identified as of fourteenth or fifteenth century character, though they were not able to decipher them. They are still quite visible, despite the blurring caused by the limewash.

As the erection of the seventeenth century south-west Bay had rendered it impossible to rebuild this doorway in its old place, it was moved a few feet further north; but the jamb-stones of its fellow opening on the east side were left undisturbed, in order to indicate the exact position of these doorways[1] to the 'Screens' at the time the Hall was built.

A piece of good fortune was the discovery, when sorting the rubble taken from the modern buttresses, of coping stones from the original crenellations of the parapet. This battlemented parapet is clearly indicated in the background of the 1624 Van Linge window on the south

---

[1]Marked 4 and 5 on the diagram, page 32.

73

side of the Chapel, where the south-east Bay of the Hall is introduced, probably as a record of its recent erection. Crenellations were fashionable embellishments at the time the Hall was built, the necessity for obtaining licenses to 'embattel kernel and machecollate,' having ceased but a few years before.[1] The form of this coping is curious and rarely found, uniting the later feature of a continuous moulding mitred around the crenellation, with the more primitive type where detached sections of coping are placed alternately on the merlons and in the embrasures. There is another example, possibly the only one, of this unusual treatment at Hengrave Hall in Suffolk.

The carved stone corbels which support the feet of the arched roof braces had been so ruthlessly hacked away to accomodate the plastered ceiling that it was impossible to trace more than the uncertain outlines of their moulded capping. They have been replaced by heraldic shields displaying the Royal arms as borne by Henry VII and George V (recording the reigns under which the Hall was built and repaired), the arms of the traditional

---

[1] Parker, 'Domestic Architecture' (part II. p. 422), records a licence from Edward IV. to crenellate Udymere manor in Sussex, as late as 1480.

VI

INTERIOR OF THE OLD HALL IN 1808

FROM A DRAWING BY PUGIN AND ROWLANDSON

founder Henry De Lacy Earl of Lincoln, and those of Ralph de Neville bishop of Chichester and first owner of the Inn. The coats are also shown of Sir Thomas Lovell, K.G. who built the Gate-house and did certain work to the Hall, Sir John Fortescue Chief Justice of the King's Bench under Henry VI and 'Gubernator' of the Inn in 1425, Francis Suliarde the Bencher to whom the first lease of the Bishop's mansion was granted, and of 'Mr. Attorney' Richard Kingsmill who bought the freehold on behalf of his fellow Benchers in 1580. In each case the authentic blazon of the coat has been obtained by the courtesy of Windsor Herald.

With very great regret, the wish of the Benchers to preserve intact the old brickwork had to be abandoned. Had it been but a question of restoring the walls to the perpendicular, means had been devised for the purpose; but they proved to be fissured longitudinally and quite ruinous. The bricks of which they were built were, nevertheless, sound and good, and after careful drawings had been made of the diaper patterns in every part, they were re-set exactly as by their first builders. Some coarse and incongrous walling, found in the modern parapets and in places where openings had

been cut in the old walls and afterwards filled
in, was removed and the defects 'made good'
with bricks specially made to match those of
the Tudor walls. The ancient tiles which had
been found were also successfully reproduced
and their pleasant texture and colour are thus
preserved in the new roof covering.

Although the primitive device of an open
fire in the middle of the floor, by which the
Hall was originally warmed, had long been
found intolerable, the building was never provided, as were many of its kind, with a fireplace and chimney in one of the side walls.
During its use as a court in the early XIX
century, a huge central stove[1] (with an un-
sightly pipe sticking through the roof) appar-
ently sufficed for our hardy forbears. This
stove was subsequently replaced by a crude
system of hot water pipes and gratings, possibly the most unhealthy form of heating ever
contrived. It is better to warm the building
itself and its occupants by radiant heat—such
as is given by the sun's rays or an open fire—
than to raise the temperature of the air within and around them by convected heat de-
rived from the clustered pipes known as
'radiators.' The principle of the Roman

[1]See Rowlandson's view, p. 74.

hypocaust was therefore adopted in the renovated building, and warmth imparted to the structure itself by a circulation of moderately hot water in buried pipes.

Many years ago, probably when the Hall was converted to the purposes of a Court, the floor had been laid with deal boarding, of which the unventilated joisting was found to be decayed and very foul. Following precedent, the dais is now floored with oak, converted from the ancient material used for repairing the roof woodwork, but the main floor is laid with west country tiles in two colours, disposed in a design adapted by the architect from a fourteenth century manuscript. Such tiles are excellent conductors of heat, and the floor takes its part in maintaining a pleasant temperature in the Hall.

* * *

Both the east and west walls of the chambers over the the old Panetry and Buttery had been for many years in a disquieting state of decay, the western wall in particular having acquired a portentous bulge of nine inches in its upper storey, besides being much out of upright. For all that, careful observations made at regular intervals during many years revealed no change, the structure having arrived at the condition of suspended equilibrium, often found in ancient buildings, which persists for an amazing time provided no disturbing cause sets them again in motion. In this case, the movement already perceptible in the Old Hall supplied the needed impetus, and the wall had to be shored for safety and rebuilt. It was decided to accept the opportunity thus offered to remove the entrance of No. 17 further South, and reinstate the old passage, which has thus recovered both its historic position and its reason as a covered entry to the Hall. This passage-way is that of 1624[1], formed, as already stated, to the south of the original screens when the two south bays were added. The stone jambs and head of the earlier doorway to the Offices, which was then built up, have been exposed to view, and the two doorways formed to correspond with the openings in the later screen have been restored to their use as entrances to the Hall. The amusing plaster ribbed groining which formed the ceiling—probably seventeenth century work—was repaired and left in position. Incidentally, it may be observed that the 'Law Notices' exhibited in this passage (the 'Screens') are placed there with historical propriety. It was

[1] See page 37.

not only the approach to the Hall, but the most frequented place in the domestic system; with a brisk traffic of guests, servants, and messengers, around the buttery-hatch, where was a wash-basin with running water—its towel hanging on a hook beside it. Consequently, if a notice had to be published it was ordered to be 'screened,'—placed where it would meet the eye of all coming and going about the business of the community.

The clock in the upper part of the Jacobean Screen dates from 1819. On removing the clumsy painted iron dial plate it was found to have concealed a carved and pierced 'shell' enrichment. The clock needed no more than a thorough cleaning, and a skeleton dial was substituted for the old plate so that the carved shell might be left in view.

The repair of the Hall being well advanced the Bench decided that the Withdrawing rooms at the dais end—the ancient 'solar' of the upper floor, from which the Governor of the community could look upon the doings in the Hall below—should be reinstated. The Council room, with the Library and other apartments, formerly occupied the space between the Hall and the Chapel, projecting westwards—into what was then part of the garden—towards the site of the present War Memorial. They were swept away when the late Lord Grimthorpe added another bay to the west end of Inigo Jones's Chapel in 1883; at which time he also faced the old North wall of the Hall with 'Gothic' stonework, and inserted a large, inappropriate, and useless, traceried window. To make room for this new feature, the Hogarth painting was removed from the Old Hall and transferred to the vestibule of the new Library. It proved utterly unsuited for this position and was presently brought back to its proper place. The window was boarded over in order to receive it, and had thus for many years been concealed from view, save from the outside where it was, happily, but little seen.

The new Withdrawing rooms are so planned as to be available for use in connection with both the Hall and the Chapel, or independently of either building. They stand on the foundations of the demolished Council rooms, which were of later date than the Hall itself.

*   *   *

Since very early times it has been the custom of the Society of Lincoln's Inn to employ their own workmen about their buildings. Names abound in the Black Books of their

BELOW THE NEW WITHDRAWING ROOMS

Carpenters, 'Dawbers' (plasterers), and Brick-
layers, with details of the materials bought for
their use. Until the beginning of the seventeenth century 'le Brikmaker' made bricks, of
excellent quality, in the Coneygarth on the
western part of the ground, and with these
were erected all the early buildings of the Inn,
including those on the South side of the Entrance court (1609), the last in which they
were used. Where important new building
was concerned, it was generally supervised by
one or more of the Benchers. We find a grant
of chambers made, in 1522, 'for the payne
and labor William Sulyarde (a famous family
name in Lincolns Inn) haith taken abowte the
byldyng of the new Gate Howse of the Inne.'
A similar grant follows in 1535 to William
Heydon 'th'elder,' who 'hath taken upon him
to have the oversight and to cause a newe
brik house to be made of thre stories high in
the postern syde thereof, towardes the goyng
owt in to the Feldes;' the building which still
stands next the Kitchen garden.

Not often is it given to an architect in these
days to carry out work, as did his ancestors, with
his own group of artisans. The greater is the
pleasure with which the writer records here
some names of the Society's men, with whom

81

he has worked 'primus inter pares' on the repair of the Old Hall, as on that of other buildings of the Inn for many years past. It has been a pleasure to associate with them and to mark their skilful handicraft and their enthusiasm.

First in order is the foreman of works Mr. W. J. Clark, who counts forty-six years in the Society's service and whose father preceded him in that honourable employ. His qualities were proved during his direction of the work of repair. To dismantle the crazy structure, which involved the handling of heavy loads with simple tackle, needed incessant care and, at times, a courageous judgement. The light protecting roof of poles and tarpaulins which he threw over the whole building, withstood the most violent storms without damage. The work has been carried to completion without accident to the men engaged on it, and Mr. Clark has every right to be proud of his achievement.

Among the others, it is right to mention the Master-carpenter Mr. Clueit, and Mr. Phillpot, the joiner. The former took to pieces and re-erected all the complex framing, receiving such assistance as he needed in straightening the heavy timbers, for which special tackle was required, from Mr. C. Kerridge of Cambridge; the latter made the furniture. Mr. Green, the stone-mason, was recruited specially for the work, as the Society's staff does not include a mason. He showed the same conscientious spirit of duty as his fellows, unseating, reinforcing, and re-setting the myriad fragments of masonry from the begining of the work until its end. The Master-bricklayer, Mr. J. W. Bagwell, and his assistant Mr. Reeves, picked and re-laid the ancient bricks one by one in the places and in the same patterns as those which they found them.

All this was true 'handiwork.' No machine-work came upon the building and, with just such simple tools as their remote predecessors used, the workmen of the Society have handled the very bricks, timbers, and stones with which the ancient builders constructed the Hall, more than four centuries before them. Nothing is new, save the mortar of the walls and such material as was wanted to repair decay, or replace what had been destroyed.

* * *

Building operations are dry work. Those engaged upon them are impressed with the fact, and have been known to impart it to interested visitors. It is to be feared that the foregoing recital of them has not escaped their inherent aridity. But, being a part of the history of the Hall, and of the Inn to which it belongs, they have been thought worth recording. Had those in charge of the work in the sixth year of Henry Tudor's reign written even such an account of their doings, with what delight we should peruse it now.

Thus it may be, when yet more centuries have passed, that the matters here related will be of interest to those whose forefathers found the ancient Hall a wreck, and left it sound and solid. The prospect would be of some encouragement to the writer, were he not better assured of the life of the building than of his book.

His Majesty the King, as Senior Bencher of the Inn, has been pleased to intimate his intention of re-opening the Old Hall after its repair, accompanied by Her Majesty the Queen, on the 22nd November, 1928.

V. BIBLIOGRAPHY.

V.

A SHORT BIBLIOGRAPHY.

Ackerman, J.
'The Microcosm of London,' 1808-11. 3 vols. 4to.

Allen, Thos.
'History and Antiquities of London,' 1839. 5 vols. 8vo.

Archer, John W.
'Vestiges of Old London,' 1851. fol.

Baildon, W. Paley
'The Quincentary of Lincoln's Inn' (Country Life, Dec. 16-23, 1922).

Bellot, Hugh H. L.
'Gray's Inn and Lincoln's Inn,' 1925. sm. 8vo.

Besant, Walter
'Survey of London,' 1902-1909. 6 vols. 4to.

Brayley, E. W.
'Londiniana,' 1829. 4 vols. 8vo.

Buc, Sir George
'The Third Universitie of England,' 1615. fol.

Cunningham, Peter
'A Handbook for London past and present,' 1849. 2 vols. 8vo.

Delaune, Thos.
'The present State of London,' 1681. 12mo.

87

Dobie, R.
'History of the United parishes of St. Giles-in-the-Fields and St. George Bloomsbury,' 1829. 8vo.

Dugdale, Sir Wm.
'Origines Juridiciales,' 1666. fol.

'Gentleman's Magazine'
Vols. LXXVII. (1807) LXXXII (1812).

Harrison, Walter
'A new and complete Survey and History of the Cities of London and Westminster,' 1775. fol.

Hatton, E.
'A new View of London,' 1708. 2 vols. 8vo.

Heckethorn, C. W.
'Lincoln's Inn Fields and the Localities Adjacent,' 1896. 4to.

Herbert, W.
'Antiquities of the Inns of Court and Chancery,' 1804. 8vo.

Hughson, David
'London. Being an accurate History and Description of the British Metropolis, etc.' 1808. 6 vols. 8vo.

Ireland, Samuel
'Picturesque Views of the Inns of Court,' 1800. 4to.

Knight, C.
'Cyclopædia of London,' 1842. 6 vols. 4to.

Lane, Thos.
'The Student's Guide through Lincoln's Inn,' 4th Edn. 1823. 8vo.

88

'Lincoln's Inn'
Records of the Hon. Sec. of (Black Books), 1897-1902. 4 vols. 4to.

Loftie, W. J.
'The Inns of Court and Chancery,' 1893. fol.

London County Council
'Survey of London' (St. Giles-in-the-Fields. I. Lincolns Inn Fields). 1893. 4to.

London Topographical Society
(Reproductions of ancient maps). fol.

Melmoth, Wm.
'The great Importance of a Religious Life considered,' 1849. 8vo.

Newton, Wm.
'London in the Olden Time,' 1855. fol.

Norman, Philip
'London Vanished and Vanishing,' 1905. 8vo.

Northouck, John
'A New History of London,' 1773. 4to.

Paul, Roland W.
'Vanishing London,' 1894. 4to.

Pearce, Robert R.
'A History of the Inns of Court and Chancery,' 1848. 8vo.

Pennant, Thos.
'Some account of London' (4th Edn.) 1805. 2 vols. 4to. (see also the 'Grangerised' editions in the B.M. and Lond. Lib.)

Royal Commission on Historical Monuments.
'London. Vol. II., West London.' 1925. 4to.

Simpson, Sir John W.
'Some Account of the Old Hall of Lincoln's Inn,'
1928. 8vo.

Spilsbury, W. H.
'Lincoln's Inn, its ancient and modern buildings,
etc.' (2nd Edn.) 1873. 8vo.

Stow, J.
'Survey of London,' 1603. fol. (see also Kingsford's
edition, 1908. 2 vols. 8vo.)

Strype, J.
'Stow's Survey with additions,' 1709-31. 2 vols. fol.

Tipping, Avray
'Hatfield Old Palace' (Country Life, 12th March,
1927).

Turner, G. J.
'Lincoln's Inn,' 1903. 8vo. (and other writings).

Walker, J. Douglas
'Short Notes on Lincoln's Inn,' 1906. VIII. pp.

Wheatley, H. B.
'London Past and Present,' 1891, 3 vols. 4to.

Wilkinson, R.
'Londinia Illustrata,' 1819. fol.

Williams, E.
'Early Holborn and the Legal Quarter of London,'
1927. 2 vols. 4to.